·THE·LOG·BOOK
·OF·
·THE·LOITERER·

Our Camp
Post Bridge. 1914

·WATCHING MY EGG BOIL·

CONTENTS

ACKNOWLEDGEMENTS

The Council of the Devonshire Association and the Editor are grateful to
Mrs. P.M. Bourke for bringing the manuscripts to their notice and for her
active encouragement at every stage. Thanks are also due to the members of the
Brown family and the Association who have helped with information, and to
Westcountry Books for their generous assistance. Members of the Devonshire
Association are continually urged to see that their work is properly safeguarded
after their deaths, and it is pleasing to produce this book as a result of
members heeding that advice.

INTRODUCTION

THERE are still people alive who can remember the time when 'holiday' meant a day out. A day's journey of a dozen miles was an event in itself, full of the excitement of travelling on vehicles that were usually only seen carrying someone else. Every yard was of interest – cottage gardens, animals in the fields, hedgerow flowers. Travel was slow – there was time to see the faces of people in doorways, even to exchange a few words, and it all added to the occasion. Such a day was indeed a holiday, something entirely different from the normal run of daily, uncomputerised living. Mark Loram, mentioned in the log, typifies such a holiday, This flamboyant character farmed Hele Farm, North Bovey, and was easily recognised in his loud check suit, tapering trousers and wide-brimmed hat. Every year he loaded his wife and fifteen children into a cart and they went off for a picnic: it was their holiday.

Dorothy Brown captures this enjoyment of the consequences of slow travel in her log of the wanderings of the family caravan "The Loiterer". If at times she repeats herself recalling the pleasure she found in the countryside it was because she never tired of it. She lived in Kingskerswell, set in a lowland valley – the wild flowers were different on Dartmoor. She could not dash up to the moor whenever the whim took her as a later generation might but must wait for the annual excursion to refresh her memory. Her delight in the simple pleasures is so typical of her day, when little changes from the ordinary and the impact of the weather were of greater significance. Sophistication and the Internet have been bought at a price.

Her log opens in 1913. Devon's two major railway companies carried visitors to Torquay and Paignton in South Devon, and to Ilfracombe in the north. Exmouth, Sidmouth, Seaton and Budleigh Salterton could be reached either by rail or by very short road journeys from the nearest station. Those who stayed preferred the coastal scene, the last gasp of Regency fashion; inland Devon was largely ignored. Some of those who lived there were aware of the potential benefit of attracting visitors; the 1905 official guide to Okehampton tried to tempt visitors to share active holidaying on Dartmoor

Nowhere in England is such a district offered to the visitor – over 250 square miles of playground, comprising ... scenery for the artist; sport for the sportsman; floral treasures ... for the botanist; historical rude stone remains for the archaeologist; legends and curious customs to be traced by the student of folk-lore; and above all ... free access to undulating miles of heath, an air which can only be described as buoyant, and picnic spots, beautiful drives and coaching trips galore.

When the Browns took their caravan to South Molton and Dartmoor, they were deliberately seeking the quiet, untamed parts, where they could be apart and follow their own interests. They were doubtless a little unusual in preferring reading, bathing and walking to strolling on some promenade. They were not interested in 'being seen', or in the superficial holiday acquaintances which so many of their group favoured; that was too like the lifestyle they had to adopt for much of the rest of the year and it was not to be extended to holidays. 'Escaping with joy to the freedom of our Gipsy life' was with great reluctance followed by a 'return to duties and conventionality'. That they could afford both time and money to holiday at all put them in a small enough minority as it was; to holiday as they did made them distinctly unusual for that time.

The Brown family

Hercules Langford Brown was the squire of Barton Hall in Kingskerswell, between Newton Abbot and Torquay. The Langford Browns were an old-established South Devon family which had acquired the Barton Hall estate in the nineteenth century. This had yielded a satisfactory income while farming was profitable, which was as well for the Hall burnt down in 1862. It was rebuilt in the original mock Tudor style as a two-storey block complete with crenellated tower and a carriage porch that dominated the front elevation, as if it had been designed for another building.

Hercules Langford Brown was born in 1866 and educated at Winchester and Exeter College, Oxford. He bought a commission in the Seaforth Highlanders Militia which he resigned twenty-five years later. Then followed long years as Justice of the Peace, parish and district councillor, church warden, poor law guardian and, from 1920, squire. He might just have remembered the profitable years of the mid-nineteenth century but had seen the estate decline with the collapse of agricultural prices under his father's stewardship and saw no reason to be any more decisive.

He took little interest in the landed estate that surrounded Barton Hall, its main benefit being the woods which supplied saleable timber and plentiful shooting, and space for raising bloodhounds and peacocks. The collapse in the income from land did not worry him as the family had long had other interests. Fishing he truly enjoyed; the long hours waiting patiently for a bite that might never come suited his solitary personality and enjoyment of quiet places. He could be as quietly creative. He wrote a book on fly fishing which was well received, and was a capable joiner and wood turner. But the social round expected of a landowner bored him, and he had few close friends.

His young wife, Dorothy (née Reed), had much in common with him. Her father was a successful lawyer in London. Dorothy grew up there and retained a house in Norwood long after she married, in order to keep a toe-hold in the world of her youth. She trained at the Slade Institute and was successful to the point of having work hung at the Royal Academy. Like her husband she preferred the solitary, intense satisfaction of creativity to shallow talk and pointless partying. She too had few close friends and later in life was regarded as being cold and aloof. A characteristic that was to be very necessary when the family took to caravanning was her insistence on everything being in the right place. Though she had understood the social life of London's professions, she must have found Devon county life strange in the extreme. It is likely that Devon's landowners found *her* a little odd when she first arrived. Dorothy would not have minded. She was twenty, just married, and had enough to do getting to grips with managing, first Fluder House on the estate, and later Barton Hall with its small staff. She knew that her marriage could not last overlong and was determined to make it enjoyable for as long as could be.

The Browns' combined independent means and lack of family or real social ties enabled them to please themselves when it came to relaxation. A ceaseless circuit of house parties would not have appealed to them. It was quite in character that they should opt for a caravan - solitary, novel, totally unconventional and even a little daring. They paid little heed to the views of others. It may have been unusual for a landed couple to go away on holiday but then their income came more from other sources; they undertook the duties of the landed gentry but did not really belong to that or any other group. It did not seem to trouble them.

The Browns were unable to have children of their own, and the estate was entailed on the eldest male relative. So when in 1916 they decided to have a family, the only route was to adopt a little girl. Theodora was two years old and had had a succession of nurses since her mother died in childbirth. The log book speaks for itself of the pleasure Theo gave to her adoptive parents as she grew up, and she seems to have been happy with them. She was initially educated at home by governesses and took full advantage of the opportunities provided by the estate. From a young age she spent countless hours working her way through the contents of the library at Barton Hall, and also enjoyed contemplative walks in the surrounding woods. Her lifelong interest in folklore began here, and in listening to her parents' experiences.

Theo also had some ability in art, which her mother encouraged. Her drawing book, reproduced at the end of the journal, shows the beginnings of that ability in the keen observation of detail. It also illustrates how families made their own entertainment when the weather was tiresome, and indicates this family's sense of humour. Some years later Theo drew the illustrations for her father's book on fly fishing, and extended her interest to wood engraving.

Caravanning

Caravanning in 1913 was so unusual that there were no firms making caravans for the general public. Langford Brown designed his own and had it built by Jury & Sons, a Kingskerswell joinery firm to whom he supplied timber from the estate. Father Jury had been a coachbuilder in North Devon before he moved to establish the business in Kingskerswell. The size and appearance of the caravan, which the Browns named 'The Loiterer', is so well described in the log, and in the photographs, that nothing further need be added here. It is unfortunate that, being a lady of her time, there is no mention of costs in Dorothy Brown's log, and none has survived in family papers.

The internal fittings and furniture Langford Brown both designed and made himself, as he was well able to do. Like many first-time caravanners since, they made some mistakes. Even slow travelling fetched unsecured china down from shelves; white paint was cool and refreshing but difficult to keep clean and they had underestimated just how much water they would need and how hard it could be to find any. As everything in the caravan was made of timber Langford took real delight in adapting and modifying for the following season, sometimes quite drastically. Racks to hold the breakables, darker paint, ingenious ways of saving and carrying water, and complete changes in the layout were all accomplished.

Dorothy also had a hand in such work. To her it was a three-dimensional work of art, as the many changes in the colour scheme and soft furnishings testify. Changing the bed covers each year gave opportunities to alter the colour scheme and the external paintwork was changed several times.

Weighing almost two tons laden 'The Loiterer' was not designed for touring. That form of caravanning lay in the future. The Browns joined the Caravan Club in 1914 and proudly flew the pennant at their site. And that was the point – the caravan of those days was taken to a site and a camp was set up for several weeks. The caravan was the heart of it, with heat, cooking and a solid roof when the weather demanded, but there were also tents to store supplies, to act as overflow accommodation, and make the space nowadays met by an awning. Even the caravan was hung with canvas to protect the paint from fading in the sun while it loitered. No wonder extra hands were needed to make and strike camp. Some of them came from the estate. Andrew Lord was the gamekeeper there and the Pages were tenants of the Home Farm. The one outsider was Dick Roach who farmed Wellpark in Crediton, as his family still does. Several forms of haulage are mentioned, and the reduction in journey times was dramatic even in so short a time as the span of the log.

Catering was of a different order from caravanning today. Provisions were taken, and there was little in the way of convenience foods. A few potted items was all the help there was in keeping foods fresh. The rest was taken as dry provisions, supplemented by local purchases and occasional deliveries from home. Regular visits led to useful contacts, like the Postbridge post mistress, Mrs French, who roasted joints to order. There can be few later caravanners who would so enjoy making jam and bottling fruit while on holiday! Cooking was done out of the caravan on an open fire as often as possible. There was always the coal-fired New Princess stove for wet days. The caravan also provided a measure of comfort – a place for Dorothy to embroider and Theo to draw, the hidden bath and, when the solitary light bulb was added, somewhere to read.

The Browns took justifiable delight in 'The Loiterer' and happily showed it off to visitors. There was a steady stream of them. Mostly they were friends or relations who came either on a day's excursion or to stay a while. Bee, for example, was Bee Brown, Langford's sister, and Diana his niece. Parties were arranged, which required the services of at least the cook from Barton Hall, and sometimes more of the staff.

The arrival of a family tends to break down formality, and Theo was no exception. It was necessary to find a pool to paddle, to swim and, in time, to row the boat that Langford Brown built for her. If nature did not serve unaided, streams were dammed until it did. Stories told around the fire (see Theo Brown's *Devon Ghosts* pp 98-9) must have absorbed the eery atmosphere. These were family holidays for fun, the more so because they made their own entertainments and needed no 'attractions'. Despite the understatement of the text, Theo's drawings and Dorothy's illustrations make the point clearly.

The Browns were a private family, with their own ideas on how life should be enjoyed. Central Devon drew them as it has so many others over the years. 'It was hard to leave Dartmoor which (or whom) we love better every year'. Through the two private books reproduced here we are able to share that love of Devon and the enjoyment the Browns found in family life.

The manuscript

The 'Log of The Loiterer' takes up the first forty-five pages of a book of 76 plain pages measuring 253x202mm. It is bound in soft brown leather and the pages are blocked in gold. Paintings, text and photographs are intermingled and very few illustrations are captioned or dated. All the text is in Dorothy Brown's hand. There are eight water-colours, five cameos and silhouettes, and 119 photographs. Many of the latter are either repetitive or of somewhat poor quality due to fading, which has limited the number that could be used in this publication.

Theo Brown's drawings fill a Winsor & Newton Heatherley' note book (90x125mm) and are done with a fountain pen in blue-black ink. The cover of the book bears the handwritten title 'The Joys of Caravanning'. The illustrations are reproduced here in comic strip form which captures the spirit of their execution.

Hugh Bodey
Poltimore

Theo Brown, aged 14.

We, Langford and Dorothy Brown
left our home, Flete House, Kingskerswell, and started for the last
time in our Caravan on Thursday
May 14th 1913 at 9.30 A.M.
We had two horses, hired from
Matthews the furniture remover at
St Marychurch, and his man drove.
We picked up Annie and Betty
Bate at Chudleigh, and about one
had lunch on the move for the first
and last time: as several of our new
and pretty plates slipped off the table
and broke. The horses found Haldon
pretty stiff climbing, we rested them
for about an hour on the top. Reached
Exeter about 5.30 o'clock where we all
had tea in the station and left Annie
and Betty. We then drove on to
Crediton which we reached late in

the evening, and all of us, horses
included were rather tired, though
we had twice hired a third horse to
help us up steep hills. We slept
in the Van in the station yard for
our first night, and had a new tea
-cloth stolen which we hung outside
to dry. The next morning early,
after boiling eggs and tea for
breakfast on the spirit lamp, we
went on with the same horses and
drove to Head Barton Chittlehamholt
North Devon, which is a mile from
South Molton Road station and
fifteen from Barnstable. There, with
the help of two other horses, the
approach being very steep and
rough, we drove into the field above
the farm, where we were going to
camp for the summer, and which
was quite near the rivers Mole and
Taw where Langford had some fishing.
The Caravan was very heavily laded and
weighed 2 tons on the road, driver included

*Two horses could pull 'The Loiterer' on level
macadamed roads: note the lamps.*

'The Loiterer' camped, its paintwork protected by canvas and every window open.

We lived on and off in the Van through a very beautiful through dry summer 'till Wednesday, October 22nd. On the even-ing of the day before, our Van was moved out of the field in read-iness to start the next morning, and in doing so the Van got a nasty scratch going through a gate, in fact was hung up on the gate hook and had to be jacked out. What little damage was done, was afterwards very easily rectified. On the 22nd we started home being pulled by two of Mrs Manning's horses (she farms Head Barton) and driven by her son. We sent on our tents by rail, had little coal and travelled altogether as light as possible. We arrived at Crediton in the after-noon and dove into a field beyond the station belonging to a farmer called Roach, who was very obliging and let us have water milk and eggs etc: offering us fire wood.

We dined in the town that night, and next morning Mr Page a farmer tenant of Langford's came with two horses and drove us onto Haldon. We had some trouble in finding a horse to help us up the long hill, and explored Kenton in the company of a kind hearted stranger to do so. At last we procured a horse and drove up quite comfortably. Then on the top of the hill near the Race Course we camped for the night. We found no water, so had to buy 1d buckets from the people living at the Pavilion. Haldon looked beautiful in the morning it was rather cold, but the sun shone brightly. Page, who had slept at Kenton came with his horses early and started us off on our last days journey home. We were met at Chudleigh by Father and Mother in their motor, and picked up Langford's Aunt Emily at Newton Abbot carrying her with us to Fluder which we reached safely about teatime.

Nelly Forestier, who stayed
with us for a short time in
September 1913, and slept
at the farm near,
being made to work!

Our Caravan was built in the spring
of 1913 by Jury and Son of Kings-
-kerswell to our design and plans
chiefly Langford's of course.
It is 18ft long by 6ft 10½ wide, and is
made of Mahogony which is varnish
-ed on the outside, so that the beau-
-tiful grain is shown off to its best
advantage; the inside is just oiled,
which makes it a very pleasant
colour. The wheels and painted
parts are bright scarlet, and the
handles of doors, window catches
etc: are of brass. The roof outside

is painted white, inside it is left its
natural colour just varnished, it is
lighter than the mahogony as it is three
ply wood. Inside the Caravan in its
first year we had furniture made by
Langford. There was a dressing table
with cupboard underneath and a
looking glass fixed into the wall above,
next to this was a wash stand, also
with cupboard and both painted white.
We had a double bed with a spring
mattress, and underneath were our
wardrobes also of wood painted white.
In the middle of the Van is one large
table to seat four easily, which lets
down if we wish flat to the wall, and
which is covered with a cotton table cloth
of red pattern on a white ground.
We had at first a large box seat
with a rose red cushion on it, which
would seat two people in comfort, it
had a folding back and was made by
Langford also and painted white and
was intended to hold the harness when
not in use. Besides this we had folding
chairs and a rose red carpet stool.
The Van has two corner cupboards each
devided into two parts, in one side

7

is kept our food and groceries, in the
other china and cooking and cleaning
utensils. We have a jolly little coal
cooking stove, called the "New Princess"
No 6, we are very fond of her, she uses
little coal, lights easily, and her oven
quickly gets hot, and the Van soon
gets warm. The stove has a copper
pipe and copper is fixed behind
against the wall, this we soon found
to be unecessary but have not altered it.
Over the table at first we had a shelf
for books which afterwards Langford
altered, also in the corner by the bed
head is another shelf. There are
windows each end of the Van and
two long narrow ones on one side
all of which are casement windows
to open, they are curtained with deep
rose red curtains, the bed also has
a rose coloured coverlet. Along the
whole of one side over the windows
runs a rack, which we find of the
greatest use, at first this was paint
-ed white and therefore rather cons
-spicious and easily showed finger

marks. In the floor, which at first was covered with green and white linoleum, is a trap door, which when lifted up reveals a comfortable sized bath, this has a p gin it so that the water can run away under the Van through an india-rubber pipe, our wash-stand basin also emptys in the same way. Outside the door of the Caravan in the little platform is another small trap door opening into a large box where we keep our coal, and this has also an opening at the bottom where it is easy to shovel the coal out. On the right hand of the door is Langford's rod box which runs right along the whole length of the Van underneath, so that he can push his fishing rods in without having to take them to pieces

In the spring of 1914 we were busy making alterations and improve -ments to "The Loiterer" as we then named our Caravan, and paint -ed the name in large white letters on a brown ground, which was fixed up on the front of the Van. Langford made entirely new furniture for the interior of the same mahogany as the rest of the Van; a dressing table and wash stand, joined side by side each having a lid which shuts down on the top, making a most useful side board. We took the spring mattress away, for the sake of lessen -ing weight, and had instead just steele lattis which we found a great deal more comfortable and convenient. Langford made also two new wardrobes fixed under the bed, each has four trays made of three ply wood faced with ½ inch mahogany, so that they are very much lighter indeed than our first moveable cupboards of deal. He made too a charming little mahogany cupboard

in the corner by the foot of the bed,
in which we keep our writing materials.
The book shelf he enlarged and
improved making a folding bar to
prevents the books falling out on a
journey. We did away with the heavy
box seat altogether, and had instead
light folding chairs. The rack was
painted dark brown which we find
an improvement on last year's white,
and we bought a strip of rose red
carpet which was laid on the floor
of the Van so that it can easily
be removed daily for cleaning.
I painted two figure panals in oils
which might be called "Conventionality
and "Unconventionality" and which
Lingford fixed on each side of the
looking glass. Outside the Loiterer
was varnished all over the mahogony
and shutes were put up along under
the roof, with pipes attached so that
the rain water would run along them
and into buckets, to be caught, if we
wished. We joined the Caravan Club
and when living in our Van always
fly their flag, a pointed scarlet one
with white letters on it. C. V. C.

On Thursday April 16th 1914 we start
-ed off in the Loiterer to North
Devon being driven by Page and
pulled by two of his horses. We pick
-ed up Annie and Betty Bate at
Chudleigh as before, and stopped for
lunch there. At the bottom of the hill
a third horse met us after lunch
and helped us up to the top of
Haldon, which we reached about
3.30 and put the Van in the
same place opposite the Pavilion
where we camped last autumn.
There Annie and Betty were met by
their trap and left us. We found
water this time but only used it for
washing purposes as we had drinking
water with us. Before going to bed
we noticed a very large fire in the
heather which made us at first a
little anxious that it might spread
but later we realised it was a very
long way from us. Early in the morn
-ing about four o'clock we were awaken
-ed by a loud knock on the Van and
a man's voice asked if we had seen

'Escaping with joy to the freedom of our gipsy life.'

The Caravan Club pennant on the roof of the shrouded caravan.

two boys, as they had escaped from the Exeter Asylum, and he and others had been looking for them all night. Page came for us about ten and we started off for Crediton. We did not have a very pleasant journey as the dust was very bad indeed, and there was a high wind which blew the dust everywhere, our eyes smarted, our throats were sore, and everything was white with dust. We arrived at Crediton and put in the same field as before, quite early in the afternoon and Page left us with his horses going straight home and arriving, we heard afterwards, late at night. The next day, Saturday, was still fine, but much less windy and dusty and we very much enjoyed the pretty drive all day. Manning fetched us about 10 with his two horses and we started. The horses were not used to the harness and jib-bed once on a hill in the the town, but with a little rest they went on smoothly. At Morchard Road station about 11.30 we picked up Bee and Molly and their bags and took them with us to Head Barton where we arrived about 4.30.

We had a good deal of trouble getting
the Van up into the same field we
camped in last year, as the horses
jibbed and nothing could be done with
them at all. One of our lamps was
smashed against a wall and a scratch
made in the side of the Van, but
eventually, with the help of two fresh
horses and a cob the Caravan was
galopped up into the field in style.
Bee and Molly stayed with us till
the following Tuesday, sleeping in
the farm, and we remained on in
the Van for over a fortnight.
We came up again early in May
bringing Minnie our cook and stay-
-ed for some weeks having very beautiful hot weather.

On Saturday July 11th we again went to
the Loiterer, this time alone. We had a few
splendid summer days there though busy
ones getting ready to go on the Road again.
Tuesday evening the 14th Manning tried
to move us out of the field in readiness
to start the next morning, but after many
very unpleasant experiences owing to the
horses refusing to pull, Langford narrowly
escaped a crushed foot, we spent the
night a few feet away from our original
position. The next morning Page with
his two horses who had arrived the night
before, with a good deal of trouble pulled
the Van out of the field onto the Road
and we started on our eventful journey
to Dartmoor. We rode quietly and
easily almost into Crediton and then
turned off through Yeoford. Then our
difficulties began. The hills got steep-
-er and steeper, narrower and more
stoney, also we were not quite sure
of our way and sign posts were
scarce. At one post we took the wrong
turning, and it was downhill too,

consequently to get into the right road
we had to back the horses some distance
up hill, which was a difficult and tiresome
business. As we went moor-wards the
air became fresher and purer, the
country wilder, and heather began to
appear along the hedges. We encamped
for the night at the top of a very steep
hill some four miles out of Yeoford.
We had to borrow a horse to help us up
the said hill, as we stuck in the middle
of it the horses having pulled the Van
right across the road and each end was
fixed in a high bank. So, we were all,
horses, driver and Loiterers glad to
get to sleep very comfortably that night
on the top of the hill. Page was taken in at
a farm where we bought milk and butter
the next morning. All went well next day
we started early and had a third horse
for a short time to help us up still more
hills. We had a delightful journey to
Moreton Hampstead passing through a
small village Hittesleigh pronounced by
the inhabitants "Itchleigh"! with a nice
old house "The Hunters Inn". We had lunch

just outside Moreton and after found in
the village Lancey with Sport our Clumber
spanial and a hamper, the two latter were
put in the Van, Sport being tied to the stove
so that he could not fall out. I did some
Shopping while the other two horses which
Langford had ordered were harnessed in
front of Page's horses. We started off early
and had a very beautiful journey of about
nine miles to our destination Post Bridge
going up some very steep hills indeed, but
our four horses managed them well. Much
to our joy we held up several scorching
motor cars and bicycles for the roads were
so narrow they could not pass us, at one time
we had quite a trail of them some puffing
behind hooting others backing in front
and the conversations were quite amusing.
We reached our Camp about 5.30, so had
nice time to get ready for the night. We
were at the end of the Village beyond the
ancient stone bridge and past the Post
Office on the Moor in a place called Drift
Lane or Wind Whistle. We had a lovely
view and the river was quite near, also a
spring of water we could safely drink

Ready to set off from Fluder House.

*Four horses were necessary whenever the two ton
laden caravan had to be pulled up any hill.*

Washing done, the Browns and Sport sit down.

We were very happy indeed there, in
spite of having wet, cold, and stormy
weather all the time, and for it being
necessary that we should constantly attend
to our tents so that they should not blow
down; and we even pegged down the
Caravan with a chain to keep it steady.
We had many visitors, friends driving out
and having a meal with us, and we even
had callers from the village, everyone being
most friendly and kind. There was another
Caravan stopping at Post Bridge in which
two sisters lived with their cook, we of course
became acquainted and liked them very
much. We made a bathing pool in a turn
of the river, and bathed every day some-
-times twice or three times; we undressed
in the Van and ran to our pool in coats.
We enjoyed our bathes tremendously, but
after the first trial with Sport when he
scratched us both severely trying to
rescue us from drowning, we found it
best for him to remain on the bank and
guard our coats. We found house keeping
easy as butchers and and bakers and
greengrocers called almost daily, and Mrs
French at the Post Office kindly cooked

joints for us, and sold us butter and eggs
and milk. Two visitors came to us who slept
in a queer little outbuilding, not unlike a
caravan, joining the Temperance Hotel.
First Kathleen Laurence who stopped about
ten days, and then my old friend Dorothy
Hudson. She had not been with us many
days when war was forced on us by
Germany — on August 4th England
declared war. We could no longer think of
enjoyment and holiday making, and it was
doubtful if we should be able to get the
Loiterer home. We arranged with Page
to fetch us and had packed almost everything ready to start on August 5th
when we received a wire from him saying Government had taken one of his horses
and he could not fetch us that day.
On Friday the 7th he came and with the
two other horses from Moreton started
sadly home. The Moor looked glorious, the
ling heather fully out and it was hard to
leave it all. The two extra horses left us
at Beator Cross and Pages pair managed
very nicely alone. Going down a steep

hill by Moor Gate our shoe broke, fortunately nearly at the bottom of the hill, so we had to stop at the first blacksmiths we came to, which was in Manaton to get a new shoe; this took some time, and we watched a horse being shod which was going to the Front to fight the Germans. We had lunch on the Road and arrived at Fluder about six o'clock, Sport being very surprised and delighted to meet the other dogs and to find himself at home.

Our Camp
Post Bridge. 1914

– 1915 –

All the spring and early summer of 1915 the
Loiterer lived in the Barn at Fluder and when
we felt very 'Caravan sick' we used to unlock
it and sit in it and imagine we were living
in it. We both also made various small alter-
-ations and improvements there. The Van was
varnished all over outside and had a new
safety chain and brake block. Langford made
another corner cupboard in the left side at
the top end, in which I keep medicines and
"first aid" articles also needlework. He put
small compartments in the china cupboard
for keeping knives and silver. I painted
a border on all the rose coloured curtains of
small black and white checks which took long-
-er to do than I had at first expected. I also made
a bed covering of printed linen with a border
of rosy red. We bought a clock which was
fixed to the front end of the Caravan; and
we had a very strong light green canvas
outside cover made to protect the varnish
from the sun, as our last sacking covering
had torn to pieces.

On Thursday, the 15th of July 1915 about
10 o'clock in the morning Langford, I, and
Sport started away from Fluder in the Loiterer.
It was a bright morning, fine after rain and
we went away very happily for we had looked
forward to our holiday all the year.
Paige again drove us with a pair of horses
and we journeyed without a hitch through
Newton Abbot, where we stopped and did some
shopping, Kingsteignton, over Chudleigh
Bridge and up the valley of the Teign to
Steppes Bridge. Near Chudleigh Bridge we
met Annie Bate who had driven out, and
we talked to her a little before she drove on.
At Trusham we stopped and had lunch and
arrived at Steppes Bridge about four o'clock.
We camped at the side of the road in a
large quarry, with very beautiful woods
round us and opposite a wild and lovely
valley with the river Teign at the bottom.
We had a wonderful sunset and sat at our
door and strolled up the road absolutely
alone together and enjoying everything. We
hoped for a fine day on the morrow, but
heavy rain came in the night and in the
morning it was still raining hard.
Loram from Moreton Hampstead rode out

with three horses and starting at 10 o'clock drove
us into Moreton, a very wet journey through beau-
-tiful country which we could not see properly
because of the rain. We stopped for lunch in
the middle of the town, and fed some youth-
ful inhabitants with sweets. We left, drawn
by four horses at two o'clock and after going
through sheets and torrents of rain and mist
arrived very damp at Post Bridge about five
o'clock. There we camped in Drift Lane as
the year before, but a good deal further
away from the road. For the next three weeks
we had almost incessant rain, not a day
passed without a heavy shower or showers,
it was also very cold so that we were very
thankful to have our stove in the Van lit
every evening for warmth as well as cooking.
But what was most tiresome was the wind,
which bothered us by day and night, and
continued high and stormy for a month.
But after the first disappointment we very
soon settled down and had the happiest times
inspite of having to spend much time in the
Loiterer, and never daring to go out without a
waterproof

All July was wet, but after the first week in August the weather improved and became hot and beautiful. We enjoyed our swims, sometimes two a day, in the pool in the bend of the river and Langford made it a good deal deeper by digging out two rocks and throwing out many large stones. We also helped with hay making in fields round the Caravan. the weather was perfect for it and the hay smelt deliciously especially at night. We had a good many tea parties both inside and outside the Loiterer and also went out several times to tea in the Village not forgetting quite a good Concert.

'Scene from our door.'

On most of our long walks exploring the Moor, we found
white heather which was said to be scarce that year.
Altogether we had the loveliest holiday and were sorry
when the time came that we thought we ought to return
to duties and conventionality, especially as the weather
was still at its best and the Moor a wonderful carpet of
purples and gold and brown. On Friday August 24th
Paige arrived in the morning early with two horses
and with Loram and his pair pulled us out of camp
and on to Beator Cross. We had no misadventure
except at the start, which happened before we were
quite ready for it, in fact we were kept talking to
people who had come to see us start. I had not shut
the food cupboard and as the Caravan bumped

over the Moor onto the road, out fell butter, meat, cheese in a mixture on the floor. The butter dish was smashed and one plate which made our first crockery broken that year in the Loiterer.

We journeyed from Beator Cross with Paige only and found it tiring because of the heat and dust. One horse cast a shoe and we had to stop at Manaton blacksmith's to have a new one put on. This delayed us some time so that we missed friends who were on the look out for us on the Road, At Kingskerswell we had a third horse waiting for us and were pulled comfortably up the hill and all arrived safely at Fluder about 6.30 o'clock.

List of provisions taken with us 1915

Small bag of flour. Three tongues in glasses. One ditto herring roes (not very successful) Two tins of sardines, one pot salmon and shrimp paste, one pot of bloater paste. Three bottles of soups, ox tail, mock turtle & muligatawny. Four bottles of jam, 2 lbs pots strawberry, plum, and gooseberry jelly and 2 lbs pot of marmalade. 1 lb of water biscuits 2 lbs sweet biscuits. 1 lb tea, small tins of cocoa, of pepper, of mustard, 2 packets of salt, 1 small bottle rennet 1 packet of mixed peel, 1 lb of sultanas, 1 lb of moist sugar 1 lb of lump sugar 1 lb of castor sugar. 2 jelly packets orange and raspberry. 1 packet of

candles size 12. 6 large lamp candles, 4 carriage
lamp candles. 1 packet safety matches, 1 packet
ruby tipped. 2 tins tobacco. 1 tin "Brasso" metal
polish, 1 tin of knife powder, 1 of "Vim" for cleaning
saucepans, 1 of "Zebra" for grate, 2 sheets glass paper
1 tin of black 1 brown boot polish. About 20 lbs bacon
28 bottles beer. Dog biscuits.
We had to buy extra tea, biscuits, tobacco, matches, sugar.

Chief utensils taken with us 1915

Three aluminium saucepans one ditto ~~saucepan~~ kettle one
iron large kettle one large tin kettle and one copper quick
boiling. One large frying pan one small aluminium ditto
Two enamalled bowls. Three buckets. 1 knife cleaning board
1 soft broom 1 dust pan and brush 1 mop 1 tin tray, large
enamalled jug for water, stone jar for drinking water, basket
two wooden stools. Saw, hatchet, one screwdriver, chisel
two gimlets, two bradawls, file, hammer, sledge ditto.
spade, cold chisel, nails, screws, bolts, nuts, etc. one
jack one tommy, 3 fire bars, 1 kettle hook 2 pairs gloves
Corkscrew, methylated spirit and lamp, iron and
stand, sardine tin opener, 1 iron 1 wooden spoon.

The river dammed to make a swimming pool.

A picture that gives some idea of the suspension.

Dorothy evidently enjoyed cooking outdoors.

'Real gypsies.'

– 1916 –

The sunny morning of July 27th 1916, a Thursday, saw our start from Fluder in the Loiterer, escaping with joy to the freedom of our Gipsy life after a rather strenuous and trying spring and early summer. War still goes on, alas! though the worst really seems over; but we felt we needed and deserved a real holiday and then – life in the Caravan by our two selves is so economical! We had intended starting on the day before, Wednesday, and were all ready on that morning, but no horses arrived! owing we found out to a mis--understanding about the day. But, it did'nt much matter, and as it was a boiling day, we spent it happily in the garden with the dogs, sleeping in the Van in the stable yard, as our bed linen in the house had been packed away. We had a good journey on Thursday with no mishaps, Matthew's man, old Hannaford drove us with two horses, and at Beator Cross, Loram met us with two more, and the four of them pulled us to Postbridge.

We took Panther, our black and tan blood-hound, with us in the Caravan, he was rather scared at first, but after Newton calmed down and was quite happy and well behaved.

Lancey our man, also came with us to Bovey and was most useful in managing the shoe etc:

32

he left us there, and returned by train
We reached Postbridge safely in the evening and
pitched our camp almost exactly in the same place
in Drift Lane where we were last year.
It was a glorious evening with so cool and
refreshing a breeze, and we made the largest
and most enjoyable meal we had had for many
a day before going to bed and sleeping ever
so soundly.
We made few alterations in the Caravan in
1916, but I did some lettering which was put up
inside facing the door, a part of a sonnet by
Shakespeare   "Who doth ambition shun
            And loves to live i' the sun
            Seeking the food he eats
            And pleased with what he gets

            Come hither Come hither Come hither
            Here shall he see
            No enemy
            But winter and rough weather"

AT HOME WITH DIDO

We also invested in some rustless knives called the "No Rus" which do not stain. We have found them a great help as they only require washing like silver.

For the first two to nearly three weeks of our stay, we had the most perfect weather we have ever known on Dartmoor.

Glorious sunshine all day, and except for one stifling Sunday always a cool wind to prevent it being too hot. Of course we simply revelled in this real summer weather and steeped ourselves in sun and air all day just sleeping in the Caravan at night. Every day we bathed about one o'clock as other bathers were in eating at that hour, we did enjoy our bathes. Langford made the pool very much deeper and longer by digging out. and throwing away still more rocks and stones. We took life very easily those first weeks, lay about and read and went for short walks on the Moor, keeping

. SCENE FROM BATHING POOL .

off the roads, which did Langford's sciatica much
good. Panther also sunned himself and rolled
on the turf so that in a little while his black
back shone like satin, and in the cool of
the evenings he had mad moods when he
enjoyed the largeness of the Moor to rush
about in. He was very good though and
so obedient and soon became most popular
with the human visitors and inhabitants,
though he got a nasty bite in a fight with
two snarling sheepdog curs, which made
him limp for several days.
Towards the end of those blissful weeks
another Caravan arrived from Teignmouth
drawn by a steam engine, which caused
us great excitement. They pitched their
camp in a very public place just by the
Bridge, but convenient for getting water
and nice for the three children who padd-
-led all day in the river. We soon got to
know the family and had very nice times
comparing experiences. Their Caravan
was not unlike ours outside but much
smaller, it was a hired one, not their own.
The poor things only had a few days of fine
weather out of their three weeks, when the
rain came, torrents of it, and a very
high wind. One night was exceptionally
bad, the river, the Dart rose and rose

Latrine sited well away but a dog always near.

Chairs and table would fold but were heavy.

The interior of 'The Loiterer'. No insulation in the walls and household furnishings: note the quotations.

with an angry roaring sound. We, snug in the
Loiterer, were alright except for a small leak or so; but
the other Caravanners had a very exciting time, as not only
did their Van leak terribly and all their bedding got wet,
but the River rose right under them, so that their dog,
who usually slept there, would have been drowned if they
had not taken him up with them into the Van.

A party of people who were camping higher up the river in tents found the Dart actually flowing in at their doors, and as it still rained, they thought it time to retire so fled to the village in the middle of the night in their sleeping garments, which caused much talking and amusement the next day.

The weather never got quite so fine again but we were very happy, and doubtless the more bracing air was healthier for us, we enjoyed the cooking and eating of our meals tremendously at anyrate. We were asked to as many picnics and tea parties as we cared for and gave some in return. One afternoon we had a dozen people squashed into the Van and tent for tea as the rain came and we could not sit outside. We also attended a church bazaar and made toys for one of the stalls. A few friends motored out to see us, but petrol was scarce and dear. Father and Mother came, and George home on sick leave drove out with Bee and spent one Sunday with us, finding quite a lot of white heather, which we also had done some time before, both bell heather and white ling. An old Art School acquaintance of mine staying at Chagford, came out by coach one day and had lunch with us. We were able to stay at Post Bridge for two whole months but — at last came the day when we felt we ought to return. On Thursday morning September 21ˢᵗ Loram arrived with two horses and Hannaford with another pair. We were quite ready having spent several days packing up and tidying and paying farewell visits. This time we were especially careful to see all cupboards were firmly fastened, and the Loiterer was pulled safely off the Moor onto the Road.

We had a good journey, stopping first as usual for the mens' "lunch" at Warren Inn. It was a fine autumnal day, the heather blossom faded to a lovely brown and the gorse glittering in the sunshine. It was hard to leave Dartmoor which (or whom) we love better every year. At Beator Cross, Loram left and we continued our journey with two horses. Going down a hill, a slight one fortunately, our drag chain broke! but Langford managed to mend it. Lancey met us near Bovey and about six o'clock we all arrived safely at home.

As economy, horrid word! is what everyone is expect-ed to practise these war days, we decided in 1914 not to go to Dartmoor, but also not to lose our beloved Caravan holiday. So, we settled on a nice camping ground outside Barton Hall

looking towards the sea, and on Wednesday July 11th in the evening, Stentiford came from the village with two horses and moved the Loiterer up to Barton Hall. We took our two dear bloodhound puppies with us Dido and Pilot, they had a box to sleep in, and a little house where we could shut them in on wet days, but generally they were loose all day wandering about with us and playing all sorts of games and we think were as happy as puppies can be. On the whole, the weather was not very good as it rained a good deal and was cold but we had a very happy time.

On holiday at home, outside Barton Hall.

Gladys Brown and her two children Edwin and Heather stayed at Fluder a few weeks, so were often with us in the Van.

We cooked all our own food, and for the first time made jam in the Loiterer, most successful it was too and we also bottled fruit, it was such a wonderful year for stoned fruit. One evening we gave a dinner party to three guests, our boiled salmon was much appreciated.

We were as usual sorry when we had to return to a house, though we did not do this till Friday September 14th when we arrived back in the Loiterer at Fluder about 6.30, little Dido baying behind the Caravan all the way home.

The Browns and the bloodhound puppies Dido and Pilot.

43

– 1918 –

On Saturday July 6th - 1918 soon after lunch Stentiford arrived from Kingskerswell with two horses and took the Loiterer again up to Barton Hall to the same camp as the two previous years. The men had pulled the Caravan into the road early in the morning and we had of course been very busy for some days packing her up.

·WATCHING MY EGG BOIL·

Theodora was wildly excited, and very important over the packing of her toys, her wheel barrow, wooden horse, engine, rabbit and teddy bear. she was 3½ years old. She and I did not drive up in the Van, as I had much to do still in the house. We left one maid there and a girl friend came to Fluder every evening to sleep with her. After tea I walked to Barton pushing Theo in her little pram. it was cooler then, earlier it had been very hot. I put Theo to bed soon after in her new little green canvas hammock bed slung to irons over the feet of ours.

She looked very comfortable and fell asleep quite soon . It was a lovely evening and Langford and I enjoyed our supper out of doors so much and the wood pigeons and later the owls, talked to us so nicely . Panther was one of the family party and as he began to tear the house down we put him into, which was out of sight of his beloved master, we had to take his box out and put it on the grass near the Van when he was very happy indeed . We lived there in the Loiterer for nine weeks exactly; the weather was better than the year before though August was rather a wet month . I could get no films as there was a great shortage of them then, it was a very great pity for Theo and Panther looked so jolly play- ing about together .

On Saturday September 7th early in the afternoon Stentiford came with a pair of horses and pull- ed the Loiterer back to Fluder . We went in a regular procession . First the Van with the garden water engine tied on behind, then Langford and Panther walking, next Polly and the cart full of odds and ends, and bringing up the rear Theo in her pram with me pushing her. So without any mishap, we all arrived safely at home.

– 1919 –

In 1919, Peace having been declared, we felt we might go to Dartmoor again in the Loiterer. We were de-tained at home for various reasons till July in spite of very lovely weather which made us long to be camping out. Langford made a small cupboard under the book case in the Caravan which we find most useful to keep papers and letters in, and he also made a pipe rack. When we found we could leave home, our first business was to get horses. We tried one man after another, and all were engaged or busy with Govern-ment work, so, at last we decided to have an engine, and Mr Cull, timber merchant of Newton Abbot said he would take the Loiterer to Post bridge. The day decided on was

He wished for an early start, so we were ready in good time, Langford and I and little Theo who was wildly excited. We did not take a dog as the muzzling order was on and the poor thing would have had to wear a muzzle all the time on the Moor.

The engine was late in coming, it had two men on it, we did not start till about ten in the morning. It was a nice day not too hot. Andrew Lord came with us and sat on the box to manage the brake. We were relieved to find the engine did not shake the Van more than horses did, but its smuts blew in and made things dirty and gritty.

Cull's traction engine replaces horses.

Theo enjoying her holiday, well protected from the sun.

We had a very slow journey as the engine had to stop so very often for a drink of water, and this alone took some minutes. Then in a narrow lane we had an absolute block, as, on a slight hill we met a timber waggon drawn by horses coming down with a very heavy load behind. We had to take the engine off the Caravan which then had to be backed by hand quite a long way till a wider part of the road came, when it was possible for the timber waggon to pass. The men from the timber waggon helped but it delayed us an hour, so that it was quite seven o'clock before we arrived in our old Camp at Post Bridge. We stayed there six weeks and had some lovely weather, and we bathed in our pool and Theo enjoyed paddling and playing about in the streams and among the rocks. The latter part of our stay was unfortunately very wet, cold and windy and the day the engine came to take us home was the wettest, a really dreadful day. Theo and I retired to Mrs French at the Post Office while Langford, Andrew Lord Mr French and others struggled to get the Caravan off the ~~road~~ Moor onto the road. The engine coulddo nothing on the wet moor and had a job to get herself off the turf, and the Loiterer was pulledoff with ropes and pullys. We then started on a most disagreeable journey home. We reached Moreton hampstead about ~~three~~ where Father's motor met us and took Theo and I back to tea at Fluder. Langford and the Loiterer arrived some time later safely home . . . .

In 1920 the Caravan was pulled up to Barton Hall

early in July
same place
Kitchen where
before. The
during it
covered
canvas,
roof and
painted a
lie had in it

and left in the
outside the
.. had camped
Loiterer had
stor.., been
outside with
excepting the
the door, an
dark brown.
done to prevent

the wood cracking and then of course letting in the rain,
which had happened several times, the year before. We
were sorry to have to cover our nice varnished mahogony sides, but it was the only thing to do to preserve
the Caravan and keep it water-tight. We were very
busy that July and August as the workmen were
doing up Barton Hall, there were the electricians,
painters, upholsterers, and women scrubbers, not to
speak of chimney sweeps, and window washers so
we did not get very much holiday, but were able to

hurry up the
A...on
lighting
order we
lit by
with one
connected
it was
our

work of the Hall.
as the electric
was in working
had the Van
electric light
hand lamp
from the house,
nice. We had
married servants

to help us after the first fortnight when they had their
holiday, so that we had more time to attend to other

things. My old friend Dolly Hudson stayed with us a fortnight or so and helped very much in the arrange- -ment of furniture etc: for our possessions were being moved by instalments from Fluder. Doll slept all alone in Barton Hall in a room over- -looking the Caravan. We had fairly good weather but cold & rather a lot of rain. Early in September our furniture and goods having all been moved and being put fairly straight, we left the Caravan and slept in Barton Hall as the nights were very cold and the weather wet. After a general tidying up the Loiterer was pulled back by Stentiford as we had no place for her at Barton, to Fluder and her home.

Post Bridge again in 1921!

We had arranged and planned to go to Heatree near Manaton, but at the last moment found there were great difficulties in getting milk, so after receiving permission from Mr French to camp on his ground we decided on Post Bridge again! We hired a motor lorry from Torquay this time, it was supposed to pull four tons. On Tuesday July 26th it arrived at 6.30 in the morning. The Loiterer had been brought up from Fluder about a fortnight before by Stentiford and left outside the library window, and was all packed up and ready to start. Langford, "Lady" our bloodhound, and Andrew Lord, started off in the Caravan drawn by the lorry. Theo and I waited in the house, which we were leaving to the care of Clem and Bee and two servants. Mother arrived before long in her Car, and drove Theo and I after the Caravan, which we passed just outside Moreton. We drove on in the Car to Moreton and waited there for the Van. It was some time coming, as the irons joining it to the lorry had bent, and had to be strengthened by the blacksmith at Moreton. Then Theo and I got in the Loiterer, and Mother drove home in the Car. We had a pleasant drive to Post Bridge where we arrived in time for a late lunch.

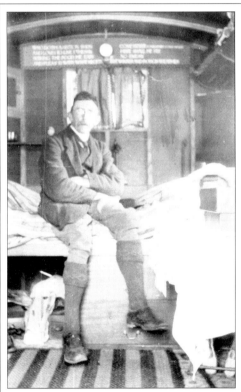

The Postbridge camp.

The family at Postbridge.

No time for smiles as the lorry is made ready for the return journey.

View from our camp.

We camped on the opposite side of the road to our
usual camp but on the Moor of course. It was a
much warmer camp and we were sheltered by a
high piece of ground but were quite near the river.
The men helped us put up our two large tents, and
then departed in the lorry taking Andrew with
them. We had a new tent, a beauty, green colour
15 ft. long. We stayed here for about a month, but
unfortunately, although it was a very dry summer
and water was urgently needed everywhere, we
had almost continuous rain at Post Bridge and it
was so chilly we lived in woolies and it was
never warm enough to bathe and Theo and I
only paddled two or three times. Langford fished
a little and caught delicious little trout, but the
river sank too quickly to allow much fishing. We
found a great deal of white heather and had many
very happy tramps over the Moor. The lorry took
us back again, a quite uneventful journey and
Theo did not seem tired when she arrived safely
at her home.

– 1922 –

During the summer of 1922 we gave the Loiterer
a new coat. From being a very dark rather unin-
-teresting brown she became a strong rich
yellow with her panals lined with dark brown
and her front board the same yellow with the
Loiterer painted on it by me in white with fresh lettering.
Her wheels, undercarriage and coal box were again
painted scarlet. Altogether we thought she looked
very smart and much improved.

Our bell tent was really done for at least as
far as Dartmoor is concerned, so we passed it on
to some Boy Scouts. Langford wrote to the same
firm who sold us the big green tent last year
and they sent us a nice new tent, smaller than
the green one, but a good size in white canvas.
The address of the firm where we bought the tents
is The Gourock Tent Co. Plymouth.

On Thursday August 3rd the Loiterer again started
for Post Bridge. We had the same motor lorry to
draw the Caravan as last year, and it came the
evening before, and was packed up with tents
and things so that it was quite ready for the
start at 6.30 the next morning. It was fine
then but not at all warm, the weather had for
some time been cold and wet, which made us hope
the more that August would be kind.

Langford went in the Caravan with Lady and
Dash, a new spaniel. Andrew Lord and his grandson sat on the box to manage the brake, and

later Langford moved there, as Dash barked so much
it was not pleasant in the Caravan.

Theo and I did not start till about 12 o'clock,
when Gladwell took us to Post Bridge in our own
little Wolsely Car. We heard the Caravan had no
adventures till she got about two miles outside
Moreton hampstead, when they met a motor
char-a-banc, whose driver refused to back.
There was no possibility of passing, and after much
argueing and waiting about ½ an hour, and
holding up countless other motors, Langford counted
though nine in front and five behind, the char-a-banc
driver realised he must do what he should have
done at once, and he backed quite easily so that
the loiterer could pass.

It started to rain when we were half-way to
Post Bridge and was raining quite fast when we
arrived just after the Caravan about two o'clock.
The men put up the tents as soon as possible,
in almost exactly the same camp as last year.
Soon after the motor lorry returned to Newton
taking Andrew and his grandson. Gladwell stayed
with us and lodged in a cottage, and the Car
was kept in a nice cart shed of Mr French's.

58

The spacious Postbridge site, where all three tents are part of 'The Loiterer' camp.

We had very wet weather almost the whole
month we were away, and it was cold.
We hardly used the car at all because of the
weather but we all drove a few times by the
East Dart for the day, where Langford
fished. He did not catch the salmon or seatrout
he wanted, but it was very pretty all along
the banks of the river.
Mother came out to Post Bridge one day
for lunch and tea and we hunted for white
heather but could not find any that day.
Another Caravan camped at Post Bridge on
our old Camp and there were several different
parties camping out in tents, which made it
interesting. But on the whole we were rather
glad to return which we did with a
comfortable journey arriving early in
September at home.

The Postbridge site had the hill for protection from the wind.

– 1923 –

In 1923 we decided to try a new camp, so as Langford was going to Scotland in August we thought we would go away in the Loiterer in June. Before we left Langford had some new wide and easy steps made to fix on to the door and they had rails. On Monday June 11th a motor lorry from Balls Newton Abbot came at 10 o'clock and loaded up and took the Caravan off with Langford on the box and Andrew and Dash inside.

Theo and I followed in the car later, and arrived at Lower Down, Bovey Tracey about 1.30 to find the Caravan had also just arrived. We had rather a business getting the Loiterer through a narrow gateway onto a private piece of moor belonging to Major Hole.

Gladwell and Andrew stayed till about six putting up tents and getting our camp straight. It was one of the prettiest places we have ever camped in with masses of foxgloves and pretty grasses all round.

'The Loiterer' camped at Lower Down, Bovey Tracey. Though the caravan had been adapted many times, the style of camping had not changed at all.

There was a dear little stream running close by the Caravan, where Theo and I paddled, and Langford made a little water-wheel which ran beautifully. We hung a hammock between the trees in this sketch, and it was always cool there. The weather was very kind, warm, but not too warm and we had very little rain. We did not go for many walks, but stayed about the camp. Our milk and butter was brought daily to us from Major Hole's farm, and the butcher and baker came several times in the week. The air suited us very well, and we all felt much better for our change. We had visitors almost every day either to lunch or tea, and all liked our Camp. Langford or I went once a week home in the car, and he went fishing two or three times to Hennock. On Monday July 2nd, a fine hot day, the lorry came about 12 o'clock. Gladwell and Andrew had come earlier and helped pack up. After lunch the lorry pulled the Van onto the road with little trouble, and arrived only a short time after Theo and I who drove in the car and about 4.30 safely reached home.

'A friendly Red Indian.'

– 1924 –

In 1924 we made a big alteration in the Loiterer,
as we took away our big bed at the end of the
caravan, and put a narrow one, and two others,
one each side of the Van. We were forced to do
this, as Theo had quite outgrown her hammock
bed. Strange to say, this change seemed to make
more room, and we found the two low side beds
comfortable to sit on in the day time.
Langford also made me a very nice hanging
cup-board inside, in the front of the caravan,
which saved our clothes being creased in drawers,
and was useful for hiding away shoes and boxes,
it was a great improvement.
The Loiterer was brought by horses, as usual, from
Fluder early in the summer, when these changes
were made, and of course the new bunks had to
have fresh covers, all to match, of greenish
cretonne, with a design of oranges and lemons.
On July the 19th, a Saturday, we went to Dartmoor
in the Caravan. We were called at 5.30! and

Langford left with Andrew and a new spaniel called Nell, about 6.30, the caravan being pulled by a motor lorry as before. Theo and I and our poodle Chock started in the car soon after 12, and arrived at the Powder Mills, which is between Post Bridge and Two Bridges about 2.30. We found the Caravan had arrived and our new camp was already being made and tents being erected. We were quite near the Cherry Brook, a pretty stream, with good water, which we drank all the time, but boiled it first. The farm was a little distance off, which we found rather troublesome, as we had to fetch our milk etc: and letters daily. The weather was not kind to us, but it was a wet cold summer everywhere. Gladwell came up twice with the car bringing Bee and Diana, and fruit and vegetables. We had one or two friends come to see us, and Theo played a great deal with a nice boy and girl, doctor's children staying near, and their boat.

On Friday, August 15th, we returned. The Caravan had a rather unpleasant journey, as she nearly turned over coming off the Moor owing to mud and water, and the lorry broke down once or twice in awkward places; but all arrived without injury except a piece of beading torn off the Caravan, safely at Home.

We made one great improvement in our Caravan in <u>1925</u>, as electric light was fitted. Just one light in the centre, charged from a battery in the box of the driver's seat. We found when fully charged the battery lasted one month.

Was it a feeling of continuity with past generations that drew the family back to Dartmoor?

Outside Barton Hall, with the steel towing hitch.

Dartmoor.

On Monday, July 20th 1925, at eleven o'clock, the motor lorry came and took the Loiterer away. Langford and Andrew Lord going with it. Theo, Chock, the poodle, and I followed comfortably after lunch, in the car, and we arrived at Lower Down, Bovey Tracey, just after the Caravan. It was a fine day, warm, but not too warm. We camped a little lower down the hill, and nearer the stream, than we had been two years before. The men helped us put up tents, and then departed leaving us three and Chock, alone.

About six in the evening Marius Forestier arrived, he was to sleep in the smaller white tent, and stayed with us a fortnight making many sketches, one of the camp which he gave me, and I have put in this book. We had some very lovely hot weather when Theo and I put on bathing things and wallowed in the stream, it was too shallow

to swim. Langford too, took off his shoes
and stockings and waded.
We also had a lot of rain and wet weather
but found the Caravan and big tent
comfortable. The car came for us, and took,
one or other, of us home, once or twice, and
for several long days on Dartmoor. The
heather was very lovely and I was able to
do a little sketching.
Langford and Theo went fishing at Hennock
and on the Bovey, and she caught her
first trout.
We had several visitors to see us, and Langford
paid some calls on friends round.
We were very tired when we first went into
camp, but soon found ourselves better for
the change and so stayed on longer
than we had intended, and did not leave
till Tuesday August 25th. The lorry came
about eleven, Andrew drove out in the car
earlier and helped pack up. We again were
fortunate, and it was a fine day.
At Theo's wish, she and I travelled in the
Caravan to Bovey, when we changed into the
car and motored home to a late lunch. Langford
and the Loiterer arriving later, safely home.

– 1926 –

In 1926 the Loiterer was painted a deep
bright blue with orange lines, and scarlet
wheels. It looked very gay, and Theo and I
had overalls o made of cretonne to match.
On August 3rd Langford and Jack Ley
started off in the Caravan about 7.30 A.m.
drawn as before by a motor lorry hired from
Ball's Garage, Newton Abbot. But this year it
was a char-a-banc, not a lorry, and did not carry
our tents etc: so well, but it was more power
-full. They reached Exeter at 11.50, Taunton about
+ 3 P.m. and had lunch outside the Inn about
two miles from Cullumpton. They stopped for
tea at Street at 5 oclock, and spent the
night outside the Three Horse Shoes at
Chapmanslade. On the 4th they started again
at 9.15 and arrived in Savanake Forest
Wiltshire, and pitched the camp at 2.15.
Theo and I started in our car on the
5th of August with Choc and Curly our
dogs, about 10.30 in the morning. It was
fine and warm and we had a very pleasant
drive stopping for lunch on the way.

We looked out for the Caravan as we
neared Wiltshire but of course found them
in camp in the Forest, but they had intend-
-ed taking three days over the journey. We
arrived rather late in the afternoon to find
two very hot tired men who had been
working hard to clean the caravan from
the soot and dirt it had accumulated
on the journey, but who had overlooked the
fact that a bottle of stout and one of
beer they had stowed away in Theo's
bunk had both come uncorked and
flooded her pillow and bolster!!
Our car returned home almost at once.
Jack Ley was with us for a fortnight
and for the rest of the time we were alone.
We had mostly fine weather and quite
warm, but also a good deal of rain,
when we found the long grass round

the camp, trying. The deer in the Forest were very tame, and delightful to watch, but on the whole we were disappointed with our camping ground. It was a private ground belonging to Lord Aylesbury and he allowed that year members of the Caravan Club to camp there. So we had hoped to meet many other caravanners there and compare notes about caravans. But only one other Van was stopping there permanently though several others came for a night or so, mostly trailers, to cars.

The same motor char-a-banc pulled us home. We started on Wednesday, Sept: 1st, all three of us and the two dogs. Theo rode in the char-a-banc a good deal of the time, Langford on the box of the Caravan, and I with the dogs inside. It was fine on the whole, and we really quite enjoyed ourselves. The first night we stopped outside a small inn at Bourton, a village about four miles from Wincanton, and had breakfast in the Inn; and the second night by the side of the road just outside Honiton and near what we thought was a nice little moorland stream, it was not." We arrived on the 3rd Friday, safely at home.

– 1927 –

*Theo and Chock
on the safer steps.*

I n 1927
we went to Postbridge, starting on Wednesday August 3rd
on a fine warm morning about 11·30 o'clock. We all three
and Chock went in the Caravan, and Andrew Lord came
also to help on the journey. We had the same lorry to pull
us as in 1925. We lunched at Reddaford Waters and got
to Postbridge about 6 o'clock. We had a slow journey as
the lorry was not working quite properly and jibbed at
the hills. We camped in Drift Lane, but on the opposite side
to our old camps. We stayed there till Wednesday the 31st,
and had very bad weather. Rain, rain, and yet rain, and tre-
-mendous winds. Diana Brown had been coming to stay with us,
but the weather was too bad. Langford had, earlier in the
year, made Theo a little boat "The Dot", just the size for her
to sit in, and it was a great success, and gave her a lot of
fun. We saw one or two other Caravans, and had a few tea parties
but on the whole had a quiet time, and felt very much better in
health at the end of it. On our journey back, in going close to an un-
cut hedge to allow a motor to pass, the canvas on one of our outside
panals was badly torn, but that was soon mended after our arrival home.

– 1928 –

In 1928 we went off in the Loiterer on Wednesday, August 8th.
It was a fine morning, and a lorry came to draw us about 10 o'clock.
Langford had to go into Newton early to an important meeting, so
Theo, Chock, Curly and I went off with the men in the Caravan and
met him in Newton. We arrived at Teigngrace about two o'clock,
and camped just by the river in a field, and near a leat
where we drew our water. The men put up the tents and left later.
We stayed in this camp for a month, but did not have very
good weather, as it was cold and it rained a good deal.
Edwin Brown came and stayed with us a short time, sleeping
in the tent. He and Theo bathed a good bit in the river and
enjoyed going in Theo's boat which floated very well. I bathed too,
but found it very cold. The Bates lived not far away, and we
saw them several times. Our car came also and we shopped
in it and had some drives on Dartmoor. It was a pretty camp
with lovely flowers about us, but we did not feel very well
and found out rather late that the water was not very pure.
On Tuesday, September 4th, a fine warm day, the lorry came and
after Theo had had her last bathe in the river, we all
travelled back in the Loiterer, and safely arrived about 5.30
without any mishaps, at home.

Dismantling the camp and loading the lorry before returning to conventionality.

Seventeen years on and Langford Brown could be pleased with his design.

We did not go away in the Loiterer in 1929 at all, but for a motor tour to the North instead.

In 1930 we decided to go. We packed poor Theo off to her school as a boarder, and went away with Chock in the Caravan drawn as usual by a motor lorry. The Loiterer had been painted light green with details of peacock blue, which looked all right against Nature's greens and blues.

We started on a lovely day in June a Wednesday, the 11th. The Caravan went first with Langford and Andrew inside. I came on later in the car, and we arrived about the same time at Lower Down, Bovey Tracey, where we had camped twice before. As usual, there was a great deal of trouble getting in at the gateway, although the post had been removed. The men put up tents for us and left about 5.30, after I had made them

> That a caravan, attached to a motor, was aptly labelled "The loiterer."
> That as the vehicle passed through Newton the two occupants were enjoying a nap.

some tea. We did not take the smaller tent.
We only stayed for ten days, but had lovely
weather, quite hot; and the song of the
birds was delightful; also the masses of
honeysuckle and wild roses in the hedges.
Theo came out for the day our first Saturday,
and she and Diana came up in the car
from their schools on the next, the 21st
'when we all returned in the Caravan.
The lorry arrived at two o'clock, and after
driving more easily out of the gateway, we
had a good journey arriving about
4.30 to tea and home.

Theo Brown's Notebook
THE JOYS OF CARAVANING

Theo filled her notebook with sketches during the pouring wet holiday in 1927. She was then 15, and tackles the holiday task with observation, humour and a surprising detachment that leads her to make as much fun of herself as of others.

The under-powered lorry struggling with an over-loaded caravan gives way to setting up camp and the first disturbed night. The site chores of lighting the stove and collecting water are followed by holiday activities, as the improving weather encourages walking, fishing, swimming and her new little boat. A hotel meal and a day with visitors make for a change before everything is packed away for the return journey. The whole story neatly fills the notebook.

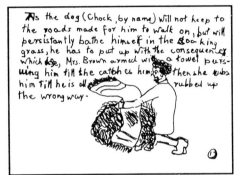

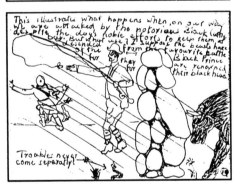

But, if Mr. Brown is hungry, I am more hungry — so much so in fact, that I find this is the quickest way to consume it! (Of course, there's many a slip 'twixt cup and lip!)

Me drinking the exquisite Mock Turtle Soup.

(23)

The dog has a sumptous feed from the food Mr. and Mrs. Brown throw into his bowl having finished their own supper. (Mr. Brown has taken off his spats but he has not changed either his stockings or his shoes — bad man)

(24)

We, (not to mention the dog) although it is streaming with rain and blowing hard, brave the freezing, foaming East Dart, rather than take the trouble to boil a kettle full of water, to fill a nice warm bath. Mrs. Brown is here seen clinging to her dressing gown and saying: Not for me! I wish I was back in my nice warm clothes — Boo-hoo! Mr. Brown is saying: I can't get out! I am saying: Ugh! It is quite warm in here!

(25)

On Sundays, when we feel too slack to get lunch ready, we stroll leisurely to the D— Hotel, where a servant meets us with a loving smile on her face, and tells us we can have lunch (hors) at 1.30, but would we place enter the lounge till then. I am trusting with the dog.

(26)

But lunch isn't ready for some time, and we spend a gloomy and awkward ward 15 minutes or so. I attempt to read a book. Several people admire the dog (who is behind the arm-chair.) There is only one young man in the picture and the others aren't in sight. Finally a gong sounds. Without much to the disproval of the dog who barks till it stops, and we troop into the ...

— dining-room. Our table is pointed out by an amiable maid and we are about to settle when —

— The amiable maid perceives Chock, and with a smile announces that dogs are prohibited in la salle à manger "By Order. The Manager."

Here is Mrs. Brown K.C. is here seen pleading for Chock and fighting his case — which she wins — and we have lunch quite peaceably. Then, the bill is payed and we march out.

Cows are driven by us every morning; that is why I have them in, rather it was the others have run ahead, so that they would not be included; this one would have liked to have escaped with the others, only it was too slow.

(30)

Having arrived, we go to fetch the milk. We are attacked on the way by a dog but they don't succeed in scrapping. 31

We reach the Post Office. We obtain our milk and letters. On the way back we pause in the road to read our letters a perfect target for — 32

— Motors of which there are many. 33

In the course of our wanderings (for we often go for walks) we sometimes come across other caravans. Of course they aren't nearly so lovely as ours! Mrs Brown demonstrating on one! 34

Of course, we now and then get visitors, some of whom we are greeting in this picture. (Note Chuck welcoming the new-comer!) The rain has abated for the while. That's why we're all looking so happy, besides the meeting of friends! 35

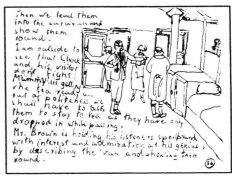

Then we lead them into the caravan and show them round. I am outside to see that Chuck and his visitor don't fight. Mummy is getting the tea ready, out of politeness we shall have to ask them to stay to tea as they have only dropped in while passing. Mr. Brown is holding his listeners spellbound with interest and admiration at his genius, by describing the van and showing them round. 36

Next we give them tea (free of charge!) Here, I am handing the lady some food, regardless of the cup of tea that I was about to now occupy by tipping over which upsets its time drink, nicely onto my lap. 37

Finally we say "Good-bye" and they depart (7.30) Mrs Brown and I are somewhere behind Mr. Brown. We are also waving "Farewell"! 38

Then in my leisure hours, I undress, put on my bathing-gown incase I fall into the river; my jersey to keep me warm; my 'mac' to keep my jersey dry from the spray; my hat to make me sunstroke-proof and I strolc down to the 'Dot' and get into her, with all her fittings fitted for a cruise. (38)

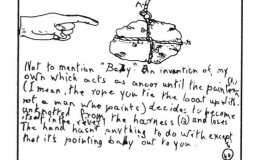

Not to mention "Baby." an invention of my own which acts as anoor until the painter (I mean, the rope you tie the boat up with not a man who paints) decides to become itself in the river, the harness (B) and loses unspotted from The hand hasn't anything to do with except that it's pointing baby out to you. (40)

This shows what happens, when I, loth to loose 'baby' go excavating for it in the 'Dot'. The result is, that I beat a hasty retreat, leaving the job till I have a bathe! (41)

During our long and tiring walks both Mr. and Mrs Brown have by their skill and observance found white heather I am here seen weeping not having found any but in (B) I am seen triumphant and content, having, by a great fluke found some! The dog is seen chasing grouse to the extreme right disappearing over the hill. (42)

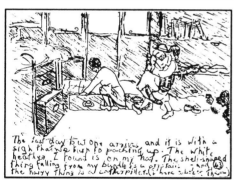

The last day but one arrives, and it is with a sigh that we turn to packing up. The white heather I found is on my hat. The shell-shaped thing falling from my bundle is a curtain, and the hairy thing is a caterpillar. (I have which is them) (43)

Having discovered that on no account are my caterpillers and grasshoppers allowed to sleep in the van, I ruefully return them to the tent. Then I go forth seeking employ-ment to help pack up carpets, straw-mats and cushions (44)

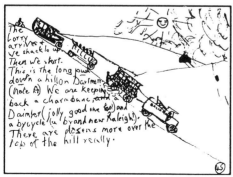

The Lorry arrives & we shackle up. Then we start. This is the long push down a hill on Dartmoor (Note A) We are keeping back a charabanc and a Daimler (jolly good too) and a bycycle (a brand new Raleigh). There are dozens more over the top of the hill really. (45)

We, Mr. Brown, Mrs. Brown, Me and Chock arriving home safely

THE JOYS OF CARAVANING! (46)

First published in Great Britain by the Devonshire Association

Copyright © 1995 The Devonshire Association and
the Executors of Theo Brown

The Devonshire Association welcomes new members. All interested in the county
are welcome, regardless of whether they were born or now live in the county.
Further information is available from the Association at 7 Cathedral Close,
Exeter EX1 1EZ. Phone/Fax 01392 52461.

British Library Cataloguing in Publication data
CIP data for this work is available from the British Library

ISBN 0 85214 053 3

Designed and produced for the Devonshire Association
by Westcountry Books
Halsgrove House
Lower Moor Way
Tiverton, Devon EX16 6SS
Tel: 01884 243242
Fax: 01884 243325

Printed and bound by The Devonshire Press Ltd, Torquay